DEVOTION
MEN IN THE BIBLE

Journey to rediscover God,
the Bible and yourself as a man

Dennis C. Stevenson Jr.

www.Dennis-Stevenson.com

ISBN: 1983693057
ISBN-13: 978-1983693052

DEDICATION

This book is dedicated to the men of the first Bible/Man Circle, and those who stuck with the journey all the way to the end.

CONTENTS

1
GET READY

IT'S-A SAD TRUTH that the Christian life is full of ups and downs. Some days we feel like God is so close we could touch Him. Other days, we can't see Him at all.

When we find ourselves in the spiritual desert, we want is to feel alive again. Memories of mountaintop experiences can haunt us, suggesting that we've fallen from God's favor into spiritual no man's land.

If you want more, if you want a vital life that's full of God, then you've come to the right place. We've been given everything we need to live dynamic spiritual lives. We just need to put ourselves in the right position to receive what God desires for us.

In this book, we'll start with stories of men in the Bible. God's stories. Stories meant for us. These stories bring spiritual life and power to bear on our lives.

If you've tried reading your Bible, but it seems dry and empty, that's no problem. This book will show you a way to read your Bible that will make the stories come to life, pull you in and breathe new life into your situation.

Of course, new results demand new methods. This book will show you some innovative techniques to use with your Bible. These techniques center around six questions that you'll investigate for each story.

Questions will lead you to answers. Answers will lead you to insights. Insights will produce passion, energy, and vitality in your spiritual life.

Are you ready?

Before you launch, let me explain the questions and how they work. They aren't hard, and it won't take long. Once you know the questions, you'll be ready to go!

I've selected thirty stories from the Bible. These stories are perfect for using the six question approach. They touch on all sorts of topics that are on-point today:

- Passivity
- Fear
- Anger
- Lust
- Faithfulness
- Trust
- Pride

… just to name a few. As you engage, the questions will focus on the areas of your life that need attention.

Jump in! As you learn the process, it will become easy, almost second nature. You have thirty stories already prepared for you. Take advantage of them and re-discover your spiritual passion along the way.

I encourage you to go to my website where you can download a workbook that will make it really easy to answer the questions for each story. It has the same stories as in this book, but I've provided a format so you can write out your answers to the questions.

You can download your devotional workbook by pointing your browser at:

https://www.dennis-stevenson.com/devotion-men-in-the-bible-workbook/

Buckle up! This is where the fun really starts.

2
STARTING THE PROCESS

STARTING IS EASY. Just read the story. The stories themselves are pretty short. You can probably knock it out in just a few minutes.

Since you're parachuting into these stories – which are all part of a larger story, I've provided a little background to set the context. In most cases, I've just tried to summarize the scenario of what's been going on around the story itself

In order to read the stories, you'll need a Bible. I encourage you to find a Bible that uses a modern language translation. I would recommend something like:

- New American Standard (NASB)
- New International Version (NIV)
- New King James Version (NKJV)
- English Standard Version (ESV)

Each of these translations will provide an easy reading translation that remains true to the original writings. As you'll soon see, the details matter. You will want a translation that keeps as many of the specifics in play as possible.

If you don't have one, you might invest in a copy of your own just for this purpose.

Take your time reading the story. Read it slowly and carefully so you don't miss anything. If you knew the story ahead of time, don't assume you have it down and go too fast.

I recommend reading the story out loud. Not only does this make you slow down, but it gives the benefit of hearing the words spoken. You might feel a little funny doing this, but trust me, it's worth it.

Of course, if you chose to do your devotional at the corner coffee shop, reading out loud might not be an option. If that's the case, you should read it slowly and carefully to yourself – or move someplace more private.

3
WHAT DOES THE CAMERA SEE?

AFTER YOU'VE READ through the story a few times, you're ready to start processing what happened. We want to start to focus on the actual data that is communicated in the text.

It's very tempting to "read between the lines." Often when reading your brain will make assumptions or connect the dots of what's going on. You will want to resist this. Instead, focus on understanding the story the way it was communicated.

Let's illustrate this with an example.

If you and I were sitting together having a conversation and my stomach growled loudly, you might be tempted to think, "Wow, Dennis must be really hungry!" That's not data, it's the story you're telling yourself about what's going on around you.

The data was that my stomach growled. There is no data for why it made such a noise. I might be hungry. But I might have had pepperoni pizza for breakfast and it could be upset. You have no way of knowing.

Paying attention to the data means staying focused on what's happening in the story. If you pay attention to the data of my grumbly stomach, then you're well positioned to also notice how I reacted to it. You will pick up on the details of what I'm eating or drinking at the time, and even if I look well or am behaving strangely.

Focusing on data means noticing what a camera would have captured. As you read through the story, think about it as a video that is playing out.

What does the camera actually see? This boils down to the actual things that we are told in the narrative and the dialog.

Focusing on data when you read the story is a discipline. At first, it will seem strange. It might even be difficult for you. Hang in there. The goal is to be grounded in the real story, not what you think the story is about.

A great practice challenge is to jot down as many pieces of data as you can about the story. No reading between the lines, just the data that the story provides. If you put some effort into this, you might be surprised at how much you can learn about the story that you never would have noticed on a quick first read.

When you focus on data, you are oriented on truth. You are working with what God has chosen to reveal to you. Data takes us out of our own heads and gets us focused on God. Good things flow from this.

Often, familiar stories will take on a whole new meaning when you pay attention to the data. You'll notice the little bits that sort of blurred into the background before. You'll see new elements of the story because you see the actual story itself.

Not all data will strike you the same. Invariably several pieces of data will jump out. Perhaps they are details that you'd skimmed over before, and now you're just noticing them for the first time. Maybe they are the data that defines and shapes the flow of the story. Or it could be a piece of data you find especially relevant or interesting. It doesn't matter why it jumped out.

We're going to work with this data. On the worksheet, there is a place to write up to 4 pieces of data. Paraphrase the data and write it down in the space provided.

Paraphrasing the data means saying it in your own words while being true to what the data actually is. When you paraphrase you aren't adding anything to what the story says. You aren't injecting your assumptions or theories. You are simply making it your own by writing it down in your own voice.

Later on, as we process the story, you'll want to look back at the data which jumped out at you. Writing it down will help you remember what it was when you need it.

4
WHAT IS THE CONFLICT?

CONFLICT MAKES STORIES interesting. Conflict makes the outcome uncertain. Conflict is also often the source of change or transformation. In conflict, we see the mechanism for growth or destruction.

In each of the stories you'll read, there is a conflict that must be addressed. In some cases, it will resolve for the better, in other cases for the worse. The main character must find his way through the conflict.

Conflict happens when a choice has to be made. Since the choice has consequences, something is at stake. Typically, the character will either be better off or worse off as a consequence of the conflict.

You might pick an outcome you want or expect to see for a given conflict. This may be based on your own experience in similar scenarios. It may be based on your sense of right and wrong in the situation. Your job here is not to pick for the story, but to observe how the characters in the story handle the conflict.

Here is an example:

In Matthew 4:1-11, Jesus is driven into the wilderness where He is tempted by Satan. The main conflict through this story is whether Jesus would give in to temptation, or if He would resist. The effectiveness of His earthly ministry hung in the balance for how He responded.

On the worksheet or in your journal, write down the conflict. This is generally "what the story is about." As you identify the key choice that has to be made, think about the consequences that would happen if the main character made various different choices. The bigger the consequence, the more pressure is on the character.

While looking for conflicts, focus on the main character's internal conflict. There may be other conflicts present, but the one that will drive the biggest insights will be the one experienced by the man in the story.

For example, in the story of David and Goliath, there is a conflict between David and Goliath - a literal fight - but it's hard to see this as a choice with consequences. There is another conflict that David experiences that is much deeper than the fight and is centered on a choice he has to make.

I won't spoil that story by saying anything here. You'll get to it soon enough and make up your own mind.

In some stories, the main character will struggle with the conflict. In others, he will make it without seeming to think about it at all. Don't let this fool you. The story is about the conflict and it's there even if the character doesn't seem to appreciate it very visibly. Your job is to observe and identify it.

5
WHAT'S YOUR JUDGMENT?

YYOU ARE A JUDGMENT-MAKING machine. It's your nature to look at a person or a situation and draw judgments about it. It's how you're wired.

Most of the time, we keep our judgments to ourselves. That's how we're taught to handle them. They aren't generally welcome in polite conversation.

Even though you suppress your judgments, they still exist inside of you. They still exert an influence upon you. If you don't believe me, think about a boss or a co-worker who you (secretly) judge to be an idiot. How do you feel when you have to work with that person? You probably don't really enjoy it very much. That's because the judgment is in there, working on you.

You have judgments in these stories too. You'll want to get the judgment out so it's in the open. Being expressed takes some of the hidden power away from a judgment. It allows you to see how you are being influenced, and make choices about it.

Some judgments are positive. There are definitely many ways you can judge a man in the story as wise, or godly or brave. You may hold this kind of judgment about a man in the stories you're about to read.

Some judgments are negative. You are allowed to bring a negative judgment to a great Bible character. We are looking at the character's actions. In a given story, these actions may be selfish, or cowardly or arrogant. When you make a judgment about a man, it's just for the scope of this particular story. Don't think that this judgment is always true of the man.

It's important to remember that judgments aren't statements of truth. They are just how you are reacting to the situation. We all have different reactions based on many different factors. Accept the judgment for what it is.

There is no such thing as "the right judgment." There is only your judgment. This isn't a test and you can't fail. As you begin to see the data and the conflict and how the man handled it, you will naturally have a judgment. That's what we're looking for. Step into it and recognize it. It's not a bad thing.

Sometimes it's hard to judge a great character in the Bible. Moses, David, and Abraham are all great men. You might believe that in many ways they represent good examples of how you ought to live your life. It might seem that they deserve your admiration, not judgment.

The Bible doesn't whitewash its heroes. It presents them warts and all. We see them doing great things, and making dreadful mistakes. In one story you might judge a man as heroic and faithful, but in another story, you might judge the same man as selfish and cowardly.

This is normal. The negative judgment does not take away from the legacy or the reputation of the man. If you ask me, it makes the reputation even greater. Knowing David was a man after God's own heart is far more powerful when I see all the ways that David stumbled and fell short of the right decisions.

If you find yourself struggling with making judgments, try this formula. Instead of asking how you judge David or Moses or Abraham, ask

"How do I judge a man who…."

Then fill in the relevant conflict and actions from the data. This helps take the man's greater reputation out of the mix and allow you to focus in on the data of the story and how your judgments are forming.

Write these judgments down in the worksheet or your journal. You'll come back to this at a later point in the process.

.

6
WHAT DO YOUR EMOTIONS SAY?

FOR MANY MEN, the idea of emotions brings up really bad associations. Culturally men are taught very little about how to deal effectively with their heart and feelings. This was not God's divine design.

God created men with emotions. They serve a purpose in your life and my life if we will let them. When Jesus was on earth, he expressed emotions. God also communicates in emotional terms.

- When Jesus' friend Lazarus died, he cried.
- When Jesus saw the temple used as a money-making racket, He burst out in anger
- Twice God spoke from heaven to say He was pleased with Jesus
- When the angel approached both Mary and Joseph, he began by saying "Fear not"

The presence of this emotional language means that emotions are a valid part of who you are and that God understands them. So as you approach time with God, it is appropriate to engage your emotions.

Let's begin by getting a basic understanding what emotions are and what they do.

Feelings, or emotions, provide us with feedback about what's going on around us or inside us. Sometimes it's information that reinforces what we sense or perceive. More often than not, emotions give us feedback that we have no other way of receiving.

Anger says I'm blocked

Anger is an explosive and vigorous emotion. It makes us feel energetic like we have to do something to blow off steam. That's because the emotion of Anger says that we are blocked from getting something we want or believe we need.

The energy of anger is one way of preparing to take on something that is in our way. Emotionally we know that something is blocking us, so automatically the emotion begins to build up the energy to do something about it.

We can be blocked from obvious physical things, like doing something we want to do. We can also be blocked from something intangible, such as love, or respect or attention. Emotionally it doesn't matter. The emotion is the same.

Sadness says I've lost something

Sadness has the opposite effect of anger. Instead of being big and explosive, sadness makes us feel small. That's because the message Sadness communicates is that we've lost something.

Rather than fighting to get that thing back (that would be anger again), sadness mourns what is gone. This is one reason why the death of a friend or loved one is so sad. They are gone and there is nothing we can do to bring them back. Sadness allows us to mourn what has been lost.

Just as with anger, we can be sad over much more than the loss of a loved one or even our car keys. Imagine losing the respect of your peers, or the reputation of being a particular kind of person, or even the love of your spouse. Intangible things can create the most intense sense of sadness we will ever experience.

Fear says I might get hurt

Fear is more like anger than sadness in that it, too, can give us a burst of energy. But instead of knock-it-down energy, fear brings get-out-of-here energy. That's because fear is sending the message that we might get hurt.

Think about "fight or flight". Anger powers the fight side of that equation, but fear powers flight.

Fear is not shameful. It's not a guarantee that we'll be hurt. It doesn't mean that we can't take it. It's just letting us know what's going on. We get to decide if we want to run away or stick around.

Think about adrenaline junkies, they let their fear power the rush that they are looking for. I'm not saying you have to become an adrenaline junkie. But you should be aware of what fear is telling you.

Happiness says I'm aligned

Happiness is different than the other emotions in that it doesn't give or take energy. It is a deep sense of contentment or satisfaction that happens when we are in alignment with the things that are important to us.

You may find happiness as you pursue a hobby that brings you satisfaction. You might find happiness in a career that you believe in very deeply. You might find happiness spending time with people who matter to you. Hopefully, you will find happiness reading God's word.

That's just it. Happiness just says that what you are doing matches what you believe and value. Don't be surprised if you find happiness in situations where you didn't expect it. That is just saying that you're doing something that matters to you.

Shame blames it all on me

Shame is what we feel when we want to block ourselves off from feeling authentic emotions. Shame is rooted in the message that we are broken or no good. It really isn't an emotion. Sometimes it's called the anti-emotion because it's what we do to hide from emotions.

Feeling broken or no good displaces authentic emotions – perhaps because we don't want to engage with them (some feelings may be very painful). It feels like an emotion, but it's really a way of shielding or protecting ourselves.

Putting it all together

These five emotions are the basic building blocks of feeling. You can combine them in different ways to come up with all sorts of combinations. Frustration, for example, is generally a mixture of Anger and Fear. If you think about it, you'll find that any emotion can be broken down this way.

Bible stories will kick up emotions

Now you have a basic idea of what your emotions are and how they work, how can you use them while reading these stories?

As you read the story, your emotions will engage. The goal here is to observe which emotion, or multiple emotions, are being triggered. There are no right answers, only your experience here.

Let me give you an example from the same passage where Jesus was tempted by Satan in Matthew 4. After reading that story you could feel angry because Satan is clearly trying to tear Jesus down with the temptations. You could also feel sad because you sense the loss of intimacy with God due to Satan's interference in the world. Perhaps you might feel afraid that Satan is going to cause something to go wrong. Maybe you would feel happy because Jesus passes all the temptations with flying colors, and holds true to the integrity of his character. Finally, you could feel shame because you're reminded of temptations where you failed and gave in.

Every story has the entire range of emotions available. Each time you read a story, you'll have to see what emotions emerge in you. There's not a pattern or any specific expectation.

If you are new to emotions, here's a useful tool that might help you with this part. For most men, each emotion tends to manifest itself in a specific location in his body. For example, I feel sadness in the back of my head, like a headache. When I get a headache like that, even a small one, it's a clue that I'm feeling sad. Other men feel emotions in their face, chest, stomach, hands, back… It's very personal.

Start noticing where in your body you are aware of something. That might a clue to an emotion. Over time you'll learn your own body's reaction to emotions and it will help you identify which emotion you are feeling.

The goal of the process is to discover what emotions you are actually feeling. Quiet yourself and you will be able to notice the feelings. It may take a few minutes. Don't be in a rush.

A temptation you will face is to determine what emotions you think you *should be* feeling. This is not the same thing, and not what we are looking for. There is no "should" in this.

Write down what emotion you notice. In the worksheet, you can just check the box next to the emotion. Don't be afraid to pick more than one. It's very common to feel multiple emotions at the same time.

Once you've identified the emotion, write a few thoughts about what is behind the emotion. The worksheets provide a couple of lines for that. If you are using a journal, write as much as you want.

Don't give up

Noticing emotions is a skill. It will improve with practice. You will certainly practice it every time you read a story. Take advantage of other situations in your life to notice what emotions you are feeling. With practice, it will become second nature.

7
WHAT'S IN THE MIRROR?

EMOTIONS YOU FEEL and judgments you hold are responses to the world around you, but also reveal much about you. What you are judging and feeling from the story also has a place in your own life. The story is like looking into a mirror and seeing yourself.

As you read the story, certain elements will resonate with your own life. Most of the time, you probably don't pay attention to these connections. You simply ignore them. However, they are still there if you care to take the time to look.

The judgments which you hold with the most energy are generally the judgments which are already working in your life. The energy you bring to them comes from the energy you have placed in them personally.

Stop and think about it. These stories you are reading are about men whom you don't personally know, who have been dead for thousands of years and are in situations the outcomes of which are already well documented. To be able to hold a judgment about them has to come from somewhere.

That somewhere is your own life.

The same thing is true about emotions. However the story moved you to feel something, that's because that feeling was already present in your life. Most likely, there is a parallel dynamic that is going on around you. The story is creating a situation that resonates with your existing emotions.

Review the judgments and feelings that you identified. These are little windows into your life. Think about where those same dynamics are happing with you. For certain, the circumstances will be different. You're not trying to look at the circumstances, just your judgments, and feelings.

If you judged the man in the Bible story as noble, where in your life is that same notion of nobleness in play? Perhaps you are experiencing it. Maybe you are wishing that it was more a part of your life in a certain area. On the flip side, if you judged the man to be a scoundrel, where is that in your life? Are you acting the scoundrel, or is someone doing it to you?

Feelings work the same way. If you felt anger about the story, it points to an area of your life where you are blocked. Where is that? Remember it doesn't have to be the same data as what you read. It's all about the pattern. The same holds true for sadness, fear, happiness, and shame. If you feel them as a result of reading the Bible story, that's resonating with something in your own life.

This is one of the most critical steps of discovery. Identifying the connection between your life and the story is the beginning of the growth process. At first, you may find this step difficult. Stick with it and practice. You will develop your skills and find it becomes easier as you keep with it.

In your journal or in the workbook, write down the connection you identified. Be as specific as you can. The more you engage in understanding the connection, the more powerful the transformation will be.

8

WHAT DO YOU WANT TO HAPPEN?

THIS IS WHERE the transformation process kicks into high gear. You've just read a Bible story about a man; you've identified the data, conflict, your judgments, and your feelings. All of this has led to the recognition of something happening in your own life.

What do you want to happen?

For example, you might have identified that you are angry because you are blocked. The consequence of your anger might be that you are lashing out at those around you. You might want better self-control to so you don't hurt innocent people. On the other hand, you might want to simply accept the outcome of the situation and stop trying to control it, thereby releasing the block entirely.

Notice that both of these wants require a change to your heart. That's what we are driving at with this process. Given that this dynamic is going on, how do you want to change? What needs God's attention in order to happen?

God is far more interested in your heart than your circumstances. It's His will for your heart to be changed to be more like Jesus. That's what brings Him glory and delight.

If God wants to change your circumstances, He will do so. But that's in His hands. While its natural to want your circumstances to change, that's not what you are looking for at this point.

You may need to wrestle with this question a bit. Your first reaction might be to change the circumstance. Resist this inclination. Focus on your heart and how it could be changed to bring peace and harmony to the circumstance.

I'm not trying to say that you should never fight for what's right and start loving all sorts of evil. I am saying that you should look at how your heart can be changed to be more like Jesus. It may mean giving up the fight and entrusting it to God to fight on your behalf. It may mean becoming more patient to see how God allows the scenario to play out.

This application question may also help you realize that you are doing things that are causing the conflict you just noticed. Perhaps you are being selfish or hasty or stubborn and that is the source of the judgments and feelings. Now that you see these elements in yourself, what do you want to happen?

Write out what you want to happen. Use the pronoun "I", or "I want". This is your application. Make it personal. The more you embrace this, the more powerful it will be.

Be specific when you write. Be particularly clear about the parts of your heart that you want God to impact. This is your journey of discovery. Make it as detailed and vivid as you can.

9
CONFESS IT TO GOD

THE PROCESS ENDS with a heartfelt prayer from you to God, asking Him to be engaged in the process of changing your heart. This entire journey has been to get you to the place where you understand what God already knows about you. Now it's your turn to say it back to Him.

Confession in its most simple form means to agree with. A criminal who confesses his crime is agreeing with the charges against him. A person who confesses to God is agreeing with what God already knows to be true.

Based upon the application you've come up with, write down two or three things that you want to take to God in prayer. This will allow you to express yourself to God and ask Him to change your heart.

Depending on your judgments and feelings and how your application works out, you might ask God to give you patience in a specific circumstance. Or you might want to ask God to remove a particular desire that is causing you to get angry. Or perhaps you need consolation in a loss that you've experienced.

Your conviction might also be positive. You might want to thank God for a change that has happened in your heart recently. You might be grateful for the way you handled a specific situation that resonates with the story you just read.

There is no right or wrong way to express your conviction. Pay attention to your judgments and feelings, and they will point to areas of your life to focus on. Trust the process to guide you and the Holy Spirit to lead you where your attention needs to go.

While you may maintain a list of other prayer requests somewhere else, keep these prayers specific to the application you've made from the story. Write them out, then spend some time praying and asking God for what you want Him to do in your life. God already knows all of this, but He delights to hear His children ask.

10
PUTTING ALL THE PIECES TOGETHER

L ET'S SUMMARIZE THE STEPS again so you can see how they all fit together. In total there are six questions that work together to bring your attention to the parts of your life that need attention.

1. What does the camera see?

What's the data in the story? What pieces of data jump out at you?

2. What is the conflict?

What choices and consequences does the man in the story face?

3. What are your judgments?

How do you judge the main man? (How do I judge a man who…)

4. What do your emotions say?

Given everything above, what emotions are you aware of right now?

5. What's in the mirror?

Where in your own life do you hold similar judgments or have similar emotions? How is the story pointing back to your life?

6. What do you want to happen here?

Given your judgments and emotions, what do you want to happen in your life?

Be sure to write down 2 or 3 things to take to God in prayer regarding the application.

At first, these questions will be unfamiliar. If you try to remember them all, you might miss some. This is why I've given you worksheets that will help you keep all of this in line until practice makes it natural. Click here to get yours:

https://www.dennis-stevenson.com/devotion-men-in-the-bible-workbook/

The most important thing is to start!!

Getting this process in your head is good, but no substitute for actually doing it. And you won't actually do it unless you start. So that needs to be your top priority right now.

Find your spot, set your time and do it!

Yes, it will feel intimidating. Yes, it will feel strange and unfamiliar. Yes, you will have to work through the process until it becomes second nature. These are all temporary issues to deal with. In a day or two, they will pass and you will be in the groove.

Think about what would happen if God got a hold of your heart and started making changes that He wanted to see. How will you be transformed by that? How much better would your life become?

Starting is the key to experiencing all of that. So don't put it off. Nothing will be better for waiting. Everything will be enhanced by starting now.

11
30 DAYS OF
TRANSFORMATION

T HANK YOU FOR READING this far. I hope what I've written will capture your imagination and fire up your spirit. That's why I write books like this.

If you've enjoyed this book, please leave a five-star review on Amazon. Even better, give the study a try and share what has happened in your life. This helps other readers discover the book.

The remaining pages in this book are the 30 stories you can use over the next 30 days of devotion. They match up to the pages of the worksheets. I'll give you a little context, then point you to the story. In order to keep it simple, I've provided all the steps for every story, so if you're using your own journal, it will be easy to answer the questions. I've published free copies of the devotional you can download if you want more.

https://www.dennis-stevenson.com/devotion-men-in-the-bible-workbook

Don't forget to go to the end of this book where I show you how you can connect with me and we can stay in touch!

God bless you on this journey.

Dennis

DAVID AND THE GIANT
1 Samuel 17:20-51

When Joshua led the 12 tribes of Israel into Canaan, they were unable to conquer and displace the Philistines who lived in the coastal plains along the Mediterranean Sea. These Philistines were repeatedly a thorn in the Israelites' side.

In this story, a Philistine army is raiding up into the hills of the tribe of Judah. Saul the king has raised an army to meet them. The two armies are encamped on hills across a valley from each other.

The Philistine champion was a giant named Goliath. He probably stood over 9 feet tall, and the weight of his armor alone would have been well over 100 lbs. Every day, twice per day, he came out of the Philistine camp and challenged anyone in the Israelite army to decide the conflict in a single combat to the death. No man in the entire Israelite army was willing to do battle. He had done this for 40 consecutive days by the time this story begins.

PRAY – Ask God to be present with you and to reveal Himself to you.

READ –Read 1 Samuel 17:20-51, preferably out loud.

DATA – What pieces of data jump out of the story at you?

- _____
- _____
- _____
- _____

CONFLICT – What is David's conflict or choice in this story?

_____

_____

JUDGMENT – How do you judge David?

_____

_____

EMOTION – Given everything above, what emotions are you aware of right now?

[ ] Mad   [ ] Sad   [ ] Glad   [ ] Fear   [ ] Shame

_____

_____

REFLECTION – Where in your own life do you hold similar judgments or have similar emotions?

_____

_____

APPLICATION – Given what you've just written, what do you want to happen in your life?

_____

_____

CONVICTION – Write down 2 or 3 things to take to God in prayer regarding what you've just written.

1. _____

2. _____

3. _____

ADAM, EVE AND A SNAKE
Genesis 3:1-12, 17-19

God created Adam out of the dust of the ground on the 6th day of creation. Man's intended function was to take care of the garden of Eden as well as the animals that lived there. One of Adam's first tasks was to review all the animals and give them names. In doing this, he realized that they came in pairs and that he was alone.

God remedied Adam's loneliness by creating Eve, the first woman, out of his rib. When he met her the first time, Adam cried out "At last!" He recognized that she was meant for him. It was the first "love at first sight" story in the history of the world.

God gave Adam specific instructions that he was to care for the garden and that every tree bore fruit which he could eat. The only prohibition was that he could not eat of one specific tree – the tree of the knowledge of good and evil. The consequence of eating of that tree was death for whoever ate its fruit.

PRAY – Ask God to be present with you and to reveal Himself to you.

READ –Read Genesis 3:1-12, 17-19, preferably out loud.

DATA – What pieces of data jump out of the story at you?

- _____
- _____
- _____
- _____

CONFLICT – What is Adam's conflict or choice in this story?

_____

_____

JUDGMENT – How do you judge Adam?

_____

_____

EMOTION – Given everything above, what emotions are you aware of right now?

[ ] Mad   [ ] Sad   [ ] Glad   [ ] Fear   [ ] Shame

_____

_____

REFLECTION – Where in your own life do you hold similar judgments or have similar emotions?

_____

_____

APPLICATION – Given what you've just written, what do you want to happen in your life?

_____

_____

CONVICTION – Write down 2 or 3 things to take to God in prayer regarding what you've just written.

1. _____

2. _____

3. _____

ABRAHAM SACRIFICES A SON
Genesis 22:1-24

God called Abraham out of his hometown in the fertile crescent of Mesopotamia to journey to the hilly area of Judea. There God promised Abraham that He would bless him and make his descendants great and as numerous as the stars in the night sky.

As he grew older, Abraham worried that he would die childless. He wanted to see God's promise come true. So he took matters into his own hands and took his wife's Egyptian servant as a concubine. This was not God's plan and ultimately ended badly for everyone involved.

When Abraham was 99 years old and still childless, God caused his wife Sarai to become pregnant. The child born to them, Isaac, was called the "child of promise" because he was the fulfillment of God's promise to Abraham.

After Isaac, Abraham and Sarai had no other children. Isaac was their only link to the descendants promised by God.

PRAY – Ask God to be present with you and to reveal Himself to you.

READ –Read Genesis 22:1-24, preferably out loud.

DATA – What pieces of data jump out of the story at you?

- _____
- _____
- _____
- _____

CONFLICT – What is Abraham's conflict or choice in this story?

_____

_____

JUDGMENT – How do you judge Abraham?

_____

_____

EMOTION – Given everything above, what emotions are you aware of right now?

[ ] Mad   [ ] Sad   [ ] Glad   [ ] Fear   [ ] Shame

_____

_____

REFLECTION – Where in your own life do you hold similar judgments or have similar emotions?

_____

_____

APPLICATION – Given what you've just written, what do you want to happen in your life?

_____

_____

CONVICTION – Write down 2 or 3 things to take to God in prayer regarding what you've just written.

1. _____

2. _____

3. _____

GOD UN-CHOOSES SAUL
1 Samuel 15:1-34

After conquering the promised land, the people of Israel were governed by judges who arose to deal with various crises. Some judges were good, others were wicked. God used them to lead His people.

Finally, the people of Israel decided they were done with the judges and they wanted a full-time king. God told Samuel the prophet and final judge of Israel that he should anoint the man that God would send the next day.

Saul, son of Kish, was out looking for his father's lost donkeys when he visited Samuel to ask for help. Saul was tall and handsome, a physical specimen that looked the part of the King. Samuel anointed him and he was crowned as the first king of the 12 tribes.

A significant portion of the King's duty was to organize and lead the army of the tribes of Israel against the people who lived around them, to maintain the borders of their inheritance and mete out God's punishment on the nations who did not worship Him.

PRAY – Ask God to be present with you and to reveal Himself to you.

READ –Read 1 Samuel 15:1-34, preferably out loud.

DATA – What pieces of data jump out of the story at you?

- _____
- _____
- _____
- _____

CONFLICT – What is Saul's conflict or choice in this story?

_____

_____

JUDGMENT – How do you judge Saul?

_____

_____

EMOTION – Given everything above, what emotions are you aware of right now?

[ ] Mad   [ ] Sad   [ ] Glad   [ ] Fear   [ ] Shame

_____

_____

REFLECTION – Where in your own life do you hold similar judgments or have similar emotions?

_____

_____

APPLICATION – Given what you've just written, what do you want to happen in your life?

_____

_____

CONVICTION – Write down 2 or 3 things to take to God in prayer regarding what you've just written.

1. _____

2. _____

3. _____

JACOB STEALS A BLESSING
Genesis 27:1-40

Isaac, Abraham's son, had twins with his wife Rebekah. Esau was born first, then immediately after came Jacob, holding his brother's heel. The boys grew up as rivals, although they were very different from one another.

Esau was Isaac's favorite son. He was a man of the field and a hunter. Jacob, Rachel's favorite, however, was quiet and lived in the tents and kept herds of animals.

One day Esau came back to the settlement after being out in the fields. He was exhausted and famished. Jacob watched him while cooking some stew. When Esau asked for some, Jacob offered to give it to him in return for the birthright of the oldest son. Esau agreed, and Jacob gave him the stew.

After this, things went back to normal. Jacob and Esau had a fierce rivalry. Esau married two women of Canaanite background and loved to make life miserable for Jacob and Rebekah their mother.

PRAY – Ask God to be present with you and to reveal Himself to you.

READ –Read Genesis 27:1-40, preferably out loud.

DATA – What pieces of data jump out of the story at you?

- _____

- _____

- _____

- _____

CONFLICT – What is Jacob's conflict or choice in this story?

_____

_____

JUDGMENT – How do you judge Jacob?

_____

_____

EMOTION – Given everything above, what emotions are you aware of right now?

[ ] Mad   [ ] Sad   [ ] Glad   [ ] Fear   [ ] Shame

_____

_____

REFLECTION – Where in your own life do you hold similar judgments or have similar emotions?

_____

_____

APPLICATION – Given what you've just written, what do you want to happen in your life?

_____

_____

CONVICTION – Write down 2 or 3 things to take to God in prayer regarding what you've just written.

1. _____

2. _____

3. _____

JOSEPH AND THE BIG TEMPTATION
Genesis 39:1-20

Jacob had 2 wives and 2 concubines who gave birth to 12 sons. Of these, Jacob was fondest of Joseph, the first son of the wife he loved the most. Jacob gave special gifts to Joseph, which his brothers hated. On one occasion, Joseph brought a bad report of his brothers to their father.

Joseph also had dreams in which his mother, father, and brothers all bowed down to him. This infuriated his brothers when he told them all about the dreams. They understood he was saying that he was elevated above them.

In order to be rid of Joseph, his older brothers kidnapped him and sold him to some traveling slave traders. They told their father that a wild animal had killed his favorite son. The news almost broke Jacob's heart.

The traders took Joseph all the way to Egypt where he was sold as a slave. He lived in the area around the delta of the Nile where it emptied into the Mediterranean Sea. Here he was beyond the knowledge of his family, and on his own.

PRAY – Ask God to be present with you and to reveal Himself to you.

READ –Read Genesis 39:1-20, preferably out loud.

DATA – What pieces of data jump out of the story at you?

- _____
- _____
- _____
- _____

CONFLICT – What is Joseph's conflict or choice in this story?

_____

_____

JUDGMENT – How do you judge Joseph?

_____

_____

EMOTION – Given everything above, what emotions are you aware of right now?

[ ] Mad   [ ] Sad   [ ] Glad   [ ] Fear   [ ] Shame

_____

_____

REFLECTION – Where in your own life do you hold similar judgments or have similar emotions?

_____

_____

APPLICATION – Given what you've just written, what do you want to happen in your life?

_____

_____

CONVICTION – Write down 2 or 3 things to take to God in prayer regarding what you've just written.

1. _____

2. _____

3. _____

SAUL TRIES TO KILL DAVID
1 Samuel 19:1-17

After David killed Goliath and routed the Philistines, he became a national hero. His fame and glory even exceeded that of Saul the king. Since Saul knew God had deserted him, he became terrified that David would overthrow him and take his throne.

Saul tried to trap David by marrying David to his daughter Michal. He charged David to bring him the bride-price of 100 Philistine foreskins. David would have to kill 100 Philistines in order to claim his bride. David went out and killed 200 Philistines and brought back their foreskins to Saul.

When Saul saw how God was with David, Saul became even more afraid of him. Not only did David bring glory down on his own head, every task he undertook, regardless of how dangerous, turned out for the best.

Saul could not get rid of David. Because of his fame, he continued to serve Saul and lead the army. This meant that David was often in the capital of Saul.

PRAY – Ask God to be present with you and to reveal Himself to you.

READ –Read 1 Samuel 19:1-17, preferably out loud.

DATA – What pieces of data jump out of the story at you?

- _____
- _____
- _____
- _____

CONFLICT – What is Saul's conflict or choice in this story?

_____

_____

JUDGMENT – How do you judge Saul?

_____

_____

EMOTION – Given everything above, what emotions are you aware of right now?

[ ] Mad   [ ] Sad   [ ] Glad   [ ] Fear   [ ] Shame

_____

_____

REFLECTION – Where in your own life do you hold similar judgments or have similar emotions?

_____

_____

APPLICATION – Given what you've just written, what do you want to happen in your life?

_____

_____

CONVICTION – Write down 2 or 3 things to take to God in prayer regarding what you've just written.

1. _____

2. _____

3. _____

MOSES AND THE EGYPTIAN TASKMASTER
Exodus 2:11-21

Moses was born to Hebrew parents at a time when the Pharaoh of Egypt was afraid of their growing numbers. Pharaoh ordered all male Hebrew babies to be killed as a way to stem their numbers and prevent an uprising.

When Moses was born, his mother did not kill him. But since she could not keep him in their home, she put him in a reed basket and floated him out where the Pharaoh's daughter would find him. As desired, the daughter of Pharaoh had mercy on him and adopted him into her household.

Moses grew up in Pharaoh's court, even though he was born of Hebrew parents. He was trained as one of Pharaoh's sons and became a prince and a warrior. He led very successful military campaigns in Cush (modern day Ethiopia) and brought much honor back to Pharaoh.

It is very likely that Moses played the part of an Egyptian. He dressed like an Egyptian, spoke like an Egyptian, even shared much of the Egyptian outlook on life and society.

PRAY – Ask God to be present with you and to reveal Himself to you.

READ –Read Exodus 2:11-21, preferably out loud.

DATA – What pieces of data jump out of the story at you?

- _____
- _____
- _____
- _____

CONFLICT – What is Moses' conflict or choice in this story?

_____

_____

JUDGMENT – How do you judge Moses?

_____

_____

EMOTION – Given everything above, what emotions are you aware of right now?

[ ] Mad   [ ] Sad   [ ] Glad   [ ] Fear   [ ] Shame

_____

_____

REFLECTION – Where in your own life do you hold similar judgments or have similar emotions?

_____

_____

APPLICATION – Given what you've just written, what do you want to happen in your life?

_____

_____

CONVICTION – Write down 2 or 3 things to take to God in prayer regarding what you've just written.

1. _____

2. _____

3. _____

DAVID AND SAUL
1 Samuel 24:1-22

Saul repeatedly tried to kill David. The situation for David had become so bad that he fled the court and become a fugitive in the wilderness. As such, he became the captain of a band of desperate men who had nowhere else to turn.

Everything that David did received God's favor. Soon his band numbered over 600 men and represented an effective military force. But they could not make Saul leave them alone. They lived in the wilderness, often far from cities where Saul could track them down.

On many occasions, Saul heard that David was in a particular spot – so Saul gathered up his army and raced to that location to capture and kill David. Every time, however, David eluded him and got away. This game of cat and mouse continued every time Saul thought he had intelligence on where to capture David.

PRAY – Ask God to be present with you and to reveal Himself to you.

READ –Read 1 Samuel 24:1-22, preferably out loud.

DATA – What pieces of data jump out of the story at you?

- _____
- _____
- _____
- _____

CONFLICT – What is David's conflict or choice in this story?

_____

_____

JUDGMENT – How do you judge David?

_____

_____

EMOTION – Given everything above, what emotions are you aware of right now?

[ ] Mad   [ ] Sad   [ ] Glad   [ ] Fear   [ ] Shame

_____

_____

REFLECTION – Where in your own life do you hold similar judgments or have similar emotions?

_____

_____

APPLICATION – Given what you've just written, what do you want to happen in your life?

_____

_____

CONVICTION – Write down 2 or 3 things to take to God in prayer regarding what you've just written.

1. _____

2. _____

3. _____

MOSES GETS WATER FROM THE ROCK
Numbers 20:1-13

Following the miraculous Passover and parting of the Red Sea, Moses led the people through the wilderness in the Sinai peninsula. The terrain was barren and rocky, and travel was only possible from one oasis or well to the next. During most of the year, there was no running water like streams or rivers.

Arriving at an oasis or well, the priority for the people would be to fill their water vessels and see to their animals – many of whom had not been able to drink at all during the day as they traveled. Typically, the people would camp at a well or oasis so they would be able to access water for cooking and provision themselves again before setting off on the next stage of their journey.

Moses would have been familiar with the watering spots from his time as a shepherd in this region. He would be familiar with how far apart they would be and how far the congregation of Israel would be able to travel on a given day.

PRAY – Ask God to be present with you and to reveal Himself to you.

READ –Read Numbers 20:1-13, preferably out loud.

DATA – What pieces of data jump out of the story at you?

- _____
- _____
- _____
- _____

CONFLICT – What is Moses' conflict or choice in this story?

_____

_____

JUDGMENT – How do you judge Moses?

_____

_____

EMOTION – Given everything above, what emotions are you aware of right now?

[ ] Mad [ ] Sad [ ] Glad [ ] Fear [ ] Shame

_____

_____

REFLECTION – Where in your own life do you hold similar judgments or have similar emotions?

_____

_____

APPLICATION – Given what you've just written, what do you want to happen in your life?

_____

_____

CONVICTION – Write down 2 or 3 things to take to God in prayer regarding what you've just written.

1. _____

2. _____

3. _____

GOD CALLS GIDEON
Judges 6:11-32

This story happens at the time of the Judges. The people of Israel have come into the land of Canaan and begun to live there. From time to time they were oppressed by their stronger neighbors, who invaded, and sometimes occupied their territory.

Lacking any kind of central government, and being largely organized in family clans, it was difficult for the Israelites to respond when attacked like this. In times like this God raised up a judge who received the gift of God's Spirit to lead the nation of people in response to the crisis.

As this story opens, the people of Midian, have invaded and garrisoned a large armed force amongst the tribes of Israel. They took anything of value so that the Israelites had to process their harvest in secret lest the Midianites take their remaining goods and food.

PRAY – Ask God to be present with you and to reveal Himself to you.

READ –Read Judges 6:11-32, preferably out loud.

DATA – What pieces of data jump out of the story at you?

- _____
- _____
- _____
- _____

CONFLICT – What is Gideon's conflict or choice in this story?

_____

_____

JUDGMENT – How do you judge Gideon?

_____

_____

EMOTION – Given everything above, what emotions are you aware of right now?

[ ] Mad   [ ] Sad   [ ] Glad   [ ] Fear   [ ] Shame

_____

_____

REFLECTION – Where in your own life do you hold similar judgments or have similar emotions?

_____

_____

APPLICATION – Given what you've just written, what do you want to happen in your life?

_____

_____

CONVICTION – Write down 2 or 3 things to take to God in prayer regarding what you've just written.

1. _____

2. _____

3. _____

SAMSON AND DELILAH
Judges 16:1-21

Samson was a judge in Israel at a time when the Philistines were powerful and were challenging Israel. The Philistines lived in five main strong cities located on the southern coast of the land of Canaan.

While Sampson was appointed by God to be a judge over Israel, he had a very complicated relationship with the Philistines. At times he fought with them and killed many himself, but at other times he seemed to co-exist with them – going so far as to become engaged to a Philistine woman.

Sampson thwarted the Philistines through his God-given supernatural strength. This strength had been on display in several prior episodes with the Philistines. He singlehandedly demolished the gates of one city and killed a great number of Philistines who fought against him.

PRAY – Ask God to be present with you and to reveal Himself to you.

READ –Read Judges 16:1-21, preferably out loud.

DATA – What pieces of data jump out of the story at you?

- _____
- _____
- _____
- _____

CONFLICT – What is Samson's conflict or choice in this story?

_____

_____

JUDGMENT – How do you judge Samson?

_____

_____

EMOTION – Given everything above, what emotions are you aware of right now?

[ ] Mad [ ] Sad [ ] Glad [ ] Fear [ ] Shame

_____

_____

REFLECTION – Where in your own life do you hold similar judgments or have similar emotions?

_____

_____

APPLICATION – Given what you've just written, what do you want to happen in your life?

_____

_____

CONVICTION – Write down 2 or 3 things to take to God in prayer regarding what you've just written.

1. _____

2. _____

3. _____

DAVID AND THE FOOL
1 Samuel 25:1-40

Saul was the King of Israel, but David was a great man and lead his own private army of men, about 600 strong and all warriors. They avoided the cities and lived in the deserted wilderness areas where Saul could not locate them. Lacking any ability to earn a living the normal way they were forced to live off the land and off the generosity of those they encountered and to whom they provided services.

In 1 Samuel 23, David and his men rescued a city from an attacking force of Philistines. The city celebrated them as heroes. They were then forced to flee the city when King Saul heard of the event. Saul wanted to capture and kill David, so he brought his army to the city to apprehend David. Moving on, David found a new location where he and his men could camp for the summer. They were numerous enough that they have some interaction with the people who live there, but this time they were not reported to Saul.

PRAY – Ask God to be present with you and to reveal Himself to you.

READ –Read 1 Samuel 25:1-40, preferably out loud.

DATA – What pieces of data jump out of the story at you?

- _____
- _____
- _____
- _____

CONFLICT – What is David's conflict or choice in this story?

_____

_____

JUDGMENT – How do you judge David?

_____

_____

EMOTION – Given everything above, what emotions are you aware of right now?

[ ] Mad   [ ] Sad   [ ] Glad   [ ] Fear   [ ] Shame

_____

_____

REFLECTION – Where in your own life do you hold similar judgments or have similar emotions?

_____

_____

APPLICATION – Given what you've just written, what do you want to happen in your life?

_____

_____

CONVICTION – Write down 2 or 3 things to take to God in prayer regarding what you've just written.

1. _____

2. _____

3. _____

ABSALOM'S PLAN FOR GLORY
2 Samuel 15:1-14

Absalom was David's son when David became king over all the tribes of Israel. When his half-brother Amnon raped Absalom's sister, Absalom plotted and killed Amnon. Fearing the wrath of his father the King, Absalom fled Jerusalem to a neighboring kingdom where he remained in exile for three years.

Finally, Absalom's return to Jerusalem was negotiated. However when he arrived, David the King would not see him. It was David's command that Absalom live apart from the royal household and be denied access to the throne room. This left Absalom wondering about his status in the capital.

For two years Absalom waited for a change in his status and the opportunity to see his father. When David did not relent, Absalom bullied his cousin Joab, one of the commanders in David's army, to plead his case before his father and broker a restoration.

PRAY – Ask God to be present with you and to reveal Himself to you.

READ –Read 2 Samuel 15:1-14, preferably out loud.

DATA – What pieces of data jump out of the story at you?

- _____
- _____
- _____
- _____

CONFLICT – What is Absalom's conflict or choice in this story?

_____

_____

JUDGMENT – How do you judge Absalom?

_____

_____

EMOTION – Given everything above, what emotions are you aware of right now?

[ ] Mad   [ ] Sad   [ ] Glad   [ ] Fear   [ ] Shame

_____

_____

REFLECTION – Where in your own life do you hold similar judgments or have similar emotions?

_____

_____

APPLICATION – Given what you've just written, what do you want to happen in your life?

_____

_____

CONVICTION – Write down 2 or 3 things to take to God in prayer regarding what you've just written.

1. _____

2. _____

3. _____

Solomon's Prayer
1 Kings 3:3-15

As David aged and became frail, a power struggle erupted across his family about who would succeed him as king. David had many sons who were old enough to want the throne, and they began scheming and plotting for how they would take power.

Adonijah, David's son finally tired of waiting, and arranged a great proclamation of his own ascension to the throne, figuring David was too far gone to do anything about it. When David heard of this, he was furious and called his son Solomon to him, along with the high priest and military leaders and anointed him as king and paraded him around the city on the royal donkey.

David was a warrior king and expanded the territory of Israel widely and established peace across the land. Solomon inherited all of these as a young king. Yet he still had to determine what kind of a king he would become.

PRAY – Ask God to be present with you and to reveal Himself to you.

READ –Read 1 Kings 3:1-15, preferably out loud.

DATA – What pieces of data jump out of the story at you?

- _____
- _____
- _____
- _____

CONFLICT – What is Solomon's conflict or choice in this story?

_____

_____

JUDGMENT – How do you judge Solomon?

_____

_____

EMOTION – Given everything above, what emotions are you aware of right now?

[ ] Mad   [ ] Sad   [ ] Glad   [ ] Fear   [ ] Shame

_____

_____

REFLECTION – Where in your own life do you hold similar judgments or have similar emotions?

_____

_____

APPLICATION – Given what you've just written, what do you want to happen in your life?

_____

_____

CONVICTION – Write down 2 or 3 things to take to God in prayer regarding what you've just written.

1. _____

2. _____

3. _____

REHOBOAM MAKES A DECISION
1 Kings 12:1-17

When King Solomon died, the kingdom of Israel was extremely wealthy and politically influential throughout the region. However, in his later years, Solomon had fallen away from his love of God and led the people of Israel into the sinful worship of idols and false gods.

When Jeroboam distinguished himself in Solomon's service as the leader of the forced workers, God told him that one day he would be king over 10 of the 12 tribes of Israel. This was a punishment on the house of Solomon for his idol worship. When Solomon heard of this, he tried to kill Jeroboam, who then fled to Egypt.

When Solomon died, his chosen son Rehoboam became king in his place. Rehoboam did not have any of the challenges of succession that his father had. He was the clear successor to the throne and made his way to receive the honor of the people he was going to rule.

PRAY – Ask God to be present with you and to reveal Himself to you.

READ –Read 1 Kings 12:1-17, preferably out loud.

DATA – What pieces of data jump out of the story at you?

- _____
- _____
- _____
- _____

CONFLICT – What is Rehoboam's conflict or choice in this story?

_____

_____

JUDGMENT – How do you judge Rehoboam?

_____

_____

EMOTION – Given everything above, what emotions are you aware of right now?

[ ] Mad   [ ] Sad   [ ] Glad   [ ] Fear   [ ] Shame

_____

_____

REFLECTION – Where in your own life do you hold similar judgments or have similar emotions?

_____

_____

APPLICATION – Given what you've just written, what do you want to happen in your life?

_____

_____

CONVICTION – Write down 2 or 3 things to take to God in prayer regarding what you've just written.

1. _____

2. _____

3. _____

DAVID RELOCATES THE ARK
2 Samuel 6: 1-23

Long before David became king, the Philistines captured the Ark of the Covenant in a battle. They kept it for 7 months, as Israel was powerless to take it back. However, God desecrated the temple of Dagon, the Philistine God, demonstrating His power over the Philistine gods.

Terrified of God and the Ark which they thought represented Him, the Philistines sent the Ark back to Israel, along with gifts of appeasement. They put the Ark in a cart hitched to two milk cows and sent it on its way (not knowing that God had commanded that it be carried on poles by the priests). It ended up in the territory of the city of Kiriath-jearim. They people nominated a man named Abinadab to shelter the Ark, and there it remained for many years.

David, desiring above all to honor God, decided that the Ark belonged in his new capital city, Jerusalem. So he set about bringing it back.

PRAY – Ask God to be present with you and to reveal Himself to you.

READ –Read 2 Samuel 6:1-23, preferably out loud.

DATA – What pieces of data jump out of the story at you?

- _____
- _____
- _____
- _____

CONFLICT – What is David's conflict or choice in this story?

_____

_____

JUDGMENT – How do you judge David?

_____

_____

EMOTION – Given everything above, what emotions are you aware of right now?

[ ] Mad   [ ] Sad   [ ] Glad   [ ] Fear   [ ] Shame

_____

_____

REFLECTION – Where in your own life do you hold similar judgments or have similar emotions?

_____

_____

APPLICATION – Given what you've just written, what do you want to happen in your life?

_____

_____

CONVICTION – Write down 2 or 3 things to take to God in prayer regarding what you've just written.

1. _____

2. _____

3. _____

ELIJAH TAKES ON THE PROPHETS OF BAAL
1 Kings 18:20-40

In these days, the northern 10 tribes of Israel were ruled by a wicked king named Ahab and his wife Jezebel. At the same time, God raised up a prophet named Elijah to speak for Him. Elijah repeatedly condemned Ahab for his wickedness and called upon him and the entire nation of Israel to repent and return to the worship of God.

One day events came to a boil between them. Ahab had been searching all over the kingdom for Elijah. God protected Elijah, preventing Ahab's men from reporting where he was hiding. Finally, Abah sent a God-fearing man to look for Elijah and God allowed him to be found.

When Ahab finally came to Elijah, he once again accused the king of leading the nation wickedly and demanded a showdown with the prophets of the main Canaanite god Baal and his goddess consort Asherah whom Ahab worshipped.

PRAY – Ask God to be present with you and to reveal Himself to you.

READ –Read 1 Kings 18:20-40, preferably out loud.

DATA – What pieces of data jump out of the story at you?

- _____
- _____
- _____
- _____

CONFLICT – What is Elijah's conflict or choice in this story?

_____

_____

JUDGMENT – How do you judge Elijah?

_____

_____

EMOTION – Given everything above, what emotions are you aware of right now?

[ ] Mad   [ ] Sad   [ ] Glad   [ ] Fear   [ ] Shame

_____

_____

REFLECTION – Where in your own life do you hold similar judgments or have similar emotions?

_____

_____

APPLICATION – Given what you've just written, what do you want to happen in your life?

_____

_____

CONVICTION – Write down 2 or 3 things to take to God in prayer regarding what you've just written.

1. _____

2. _____

3. _____

PETER'S ANGELIC VISITOR
Acts 12:6-19

Peter, the disciple of Jesus and now an Apostle in the fledgling church had been preaching the gospel boldly. Repeatedly the Jewish authorities demanded that he cease talking about Jesus and doing miracles. Each time, Peter refused.

Finally, the authorities grew tired of Peter's preaching and stirring up the people telling them that their leaders were wrong and Jesus was the only way to God. So they arrested Peter and threw him in prison.

Herod, the Jewish ruler had Peter's fellow-apostle James, the brother of John the disciple killed at this time. When Peter was arrested, it was the time of the Passover, so Herod threw him in prison until the holiday had passed so he could bring Peter out to the people to be judged.

Meanwhile, the entire church in Jerusalem gathered to pray for Peter and his salvation from what seemed like a certain and bloody death.

PRAY – Ask God to be present with you and to reveal Himself to you.

READ –Read Acts 12:6-19, preferably out loud.

DATA – What pieces of data jump out of the story at you?

- _____
- _____
- _____
- _____

CONFLICT – What is Peter's conflict or choice in this story?

_____

_____

JUDGMENT – How do you judge Peter?

_____

_____

EMOTION – Given everything above, what emotions are you aware of right now?

[ ] Mad   [ ] Sad   [ ] Glad   [ ] Fear   [ ] Shame

_____

_____

REFLECTION – Where in your own life do you hold similar judgments or have similar emotions?

_____

_____

APPLICATION – Given what you've just written, what do you want to happen in your life?

_____

_____

CONVICTION – Write down 2 or 3 things to take to God in prayer regarding what you've just written.

1. _____

2. _____

3. _____

NAAMAN AND THE DIRTY RIVER
2 Kings 5:1-27

At this time, to the north of the kingdom of Israel lay the kingdom of Syria. At different times they were bitter enemies of the Israelites. Their armies were bigger and more powerful than that of Israel. They regularly raided down into Israel and carried off slaves to sell in their slave markets.

The kings of Israel generally dealt with this terror by paying tribute every time the Syrians came to attack. The tribute was a temporary solution to the problem but did not really blunt the aggression of the Syrians. The result was that the nation of Israel was subject to the whims of the Syrian king.

At the time of this story, the two nations are enjoying peaceful relations. However only a short time after this story, the kingdom of Syria attacked and ravaged all the way to the gates of the capital city of Samaria before God intervened and sent them away in terror.

PRAY – Ask God to be present with you and to reveal Himself to you.

READ –Read 2 Kings 5:1-27, preferably out loud.

DATA – What pieces of data jump out of the story at you?

- _____
- _____
- _____
- _____

CONFLICT – What is Naaman's conflict or choice in this story?

_____

_____

JUDGMENT – How do you judge Naaman?

_____

_____

EMOTION – Given everything above, what emotions are you aware of right now?

[ ] Mad   [ ] Sad   [ ] Glad   [ ] Fear   [ ] Shame

_____

_____

REFLECTION – Where in your own life do you hold similar judgments or have similar emotions?

_____

_____

APPLICATION – Given what you've just written, what do you want to happen in your life?

_____

_____

CONVICTION – Write down 2 or 3 things to take to God in prayer regarding what you've just written.

1. _____

2. _____

3. _____

3 MEN ON FIRE
Daniel 3:1-30

When Nebuchadnezzar king of Babylon conquered Jerusalem and the kingdom of Judah, he took all the best young men of the country captive and brought them back to Babylon where they were educated in Babylonian language, customs, and law. By this means he hoped to align the future generation of Judah with his own reign.

While they were living in the royal court in Babylon, they were treated as nobles and fed from the king's table. They were also given new Babylonian names, and their Hebrew names were discarded. Hananiah became Shadrach, Mishael became Meshach and Azariah became Abednego.

These three young men, along with another youth named Daniel (renamed to Belteshazzar) resolved to resist this influence and refused the king's food, choosing to live on vegetables and water only. God rewarded their devotion and they excelled all the rest of their peers.

PRAY – Ask God to be present with you and to reveal Himself to you.

READ –Read Daniel 3:1-30, preferably out loud.

DATA – What pieces of data jump out of the story at you?

- _____

- _____

- _____

- _____

CONFLICT – What is the 3 men's conflict or choice in this story?

_____

_____

JUDGMENT – How do you judge the men?

_____

_____

EMOTION – Given everything above, what emotions are you aware of right now?

[ ] Mad   [ ] Sad   [ ] Glad   [ ] Fear   [ ] Shame

_____

_____

REFLECTION – Where in your own life do you hold similar judgments or have similar emotions?

_____

_____

APPLICATION – Given what you've just written, what do you want to happen in your life?

_____

_____

CONVICTION – Write down 2 or 3 things to take to God in prayer regarding what you've just written.

1. _____

2. _____

3. _____

DAVID AND THE WOMAN
2 Samuel 11:1-27

David became successful and powerful as a king. As a warrior, he was without equal, and the armies he led conquered every opponent they faced. This led to David, and Israel, becoming successful, prosperous and wealthy.

As the challenges declined, David turned over the running of the armies to other men, great warriors in their own right. Instead of going out to lead his armies, he remained behind in Jerusalem while the armies fought for him.

David lived in the grandest house in all of Jerusalem. It was located at the highest point of the hill on which the city was built, and would have been bigger and more magnificent than any other home within the city. From his house, he could look out over his city and enjoy his capital. And with his army out in the field, he had plenty of time to enjoy the view.

PRAY – Ask God to be present with you and to reveal Himself to you.

READ –Read 2 Samuel 11:1-27, preferably out loud.

DATA – What pieces of data jump out of the story at you?

- _____
- _____
- _____
- _____

CONFLICT – What is David's conflict or choice in this story?

_____
_____

JUDGMENT – How do you judge David?

_____
_____

EMOTION – Given everything above, what emotions are you aware of right now?

[ ] Mad   [ ] Sad   [ ] Glad   [ ] Fear   [ ] Shame

_____

_____

REFLECTION – Where in your own life do you hold similar judgments or have similar emotions?

_____

_____

APPLICATION – Given what you've just written, what do you want to happen in your life?

_____

_____

CONVICTION – Write down 2 or 3 things to take to God in prayer regarding what you've just written.

1. _____

2. _____

3. _____

DANIEL IN THE LION'S DEN
Daniel 6:1-24

King Nebuchadnezzar of Babylon died and Babylon passed on to his son Belshazzar who became king in his place. Belshazzar threw a party and thought it would be a good idea to drink wine out of the golden vessels taken from the temple in Jerusalem. That very night Belshazzar was overthrown by an invading army from Persia. This ended the Babylonian empire and led to the establishment of the Medio-Persian Empire.

Darius, the conqueror of Babylon, then set up a Persian government across the territories of Babylon and established new Persian customs. However, he continued to maintain many of the same people in power to administer this new territory.

Daniel, taken from Judah by Nebuchadnezzar, was still alive when Darius began to reign. As a man of wisdom, he was quickly recognized and given responsibility in the new government.

PRAY – Ask God to be present with you and to reveal Himself to you.

READ –Read Daniel 6:1-24, preferably out loud.

DATA – What pieces of data jump out of the story at you?

- _____
- _____
- _____
- _____

CONFLICT – What is Daniel's conflict or choice in this story?

_____

_____

JUDGMENT – How do you judge Daniel?

_____

_____

EMOTION – Given everything above, what emotions are you aware of right now?

[ ] Mad   [ ] Sad   [ ] Glad   [ ] Fear   [ ] Shame

_____

_____

REFLECTION – Where in your own life do you hold similar judgments or have similar emotions?

_____

_____

APPLICATION – Given what you've just written, what do you want to happen in your life?

_____

_____

CONVICTION – Write down 2 or 3 things to take to God in prayer regarding what you've just written.

1. _____

2. _____

3. _____

NEHEMIAH BUILDS A WALL
Nehemiah 2:1-20

140 years after Jerusalem was conquered, there were still Jews living in Susa, the capital of the Persian empire. Nehemiah was one such person. He had risen to a position of responsibility in the palace where he was the cupbearer to the Persian emperor. In this role, he was responsible for tasting everything the emperor ate and drank.

Not all Jews were living in Susa. About 90 years earlier, a Jewish leader named Zerubbabel led over 40,000 Jews back to Jerusalem to rebuild the temple. They succeeded with the temple, but the walls of Jerusalem still lay in rubble and efforts to rebuild them had been thwarted.

Nehemiah may have lived in Susa at the court, but in his heart, he longed for his homeland. At heart, he was a Jewish patriot and hoped for the restoration of his homeland and for God to restore the Jewish nation again. Unfortunately, he had just received word of the terrible situation back in Jerusalem, and the shame of the Jews who returned to rebuild.

PRAY – Ask God to be present with you and to reveal Himself to you.

READ –Read Nehemiah 2:1-20, preferably out loud.

DATA – What pieces of data jump out of the story at you?

- _____
- _____
- _____
- _____

CONFLICT – What is Nehemiah's conflict or choice in this story?

_____

_____

JUDGMENT – How do you judge Nehemiah?

_____

_____

EMOTION – Given everything above, what emotions are you aware of right now?

[ ] Mad   [ ] Sad   [ ] Glad   [ ] Fear   [ ] Shame

_____

_____

REFLECTION – Where in your own life do you hold similar judgments or have similar emotions?

_____

_____

APPLICATION – Given what you've just written, what do you want to happen in your life?

_____

_____

CONVICTION – Write down 2 or 3 things to take to God in prayer regarding what you've just written.

1. _____

2. _____

3. _____

SAUL AND THE WITCH
1 Samuel 28:3-25

Even though God had rejected Saul as king, Saul continued to rule over the nation of Israel. However, he did so alone. The prophet Samuel, who initially anointed him, had broken off all contact and left him to fend for himself. Despite this rejection, Saul's reign lasted 40 years.

Throughout his reign, the Philistines were a thorn in Saul's side. As Saul continued to battle against the Philistines, circumstances took a turn for the worse and his situation became dire. He longed for advice, but God had turned His back, and every time Saul tried to hear a word from God, he failed. Even when he went to the high priest to consult with God on his behalf, God was silent and refused to answer.

Samuel, the prophet who had anointed him and made him king had died, so Saul found himself with no one to turn to in order to decide what to do or how to respond to the crisis that confronted him.

PRAY – Ask God to be present with you and to reveal Himself to you.

READ –Read 1 Samuel 28:3-25, preferably out loud.

DATA – What pieces of data jump out of the story at you?

- _____
- _____
- _____
- _____

CONFLICT – What is Saul's conflict or choice in this story?

_____

_____

JUDGMENT – How do you judge Saul?

_____

_____

EMOTION – Given everything above, what emotions are you aware of right now?

[ ] Mad   [ ] Sad   [ ] Glad   [ ] Fear   [ ] Shame

_____

_____

REFLECTION – Where in your own life do you hold similar judgments or have similar emotions?

_____

_____

APPLICATION – Given what you've just written, what do you want to happen in your life?

_____

_____

CONVICTION – Write down 2 or 3 things to take to God in prayer regarding what you've just written.

1. _____

2. _____

3. _____

JONAH AND THE FISH
Jonah 1:1-2:10

Jonah was a prophet of God to the northern 10 tribes in the Kingdom of Israel. His job was to speak to the people on behalf of God, to make known to them what God wished to communicate.

The nation had rebelled against God ever since the northern tribes split away from Rehoboam and the dynasty of David. However, God had been blessing the people of Israel, and their borders had expanded to the greatest extent since the golden age of David and Solomon.

Nevertheless, over the northern border, a threat was developing in the Assyrian empire. The Assyrians, based out of Nineveh (located in modern day Iraq), were a cruel people who show no mercy toward their opponents. Their gaze had not yet turned to Israel since they had been dealing with internal disputes. But it is clear that they were an emerging power that must be reckoned with.

PRAY – Ask God to be present with you and to reveal Himself to you.

READ –Read Jonah 1:1-2:10, preferably out loud.

DATA – What pieces of data jump out of the story at you?

- _____
- _____
- _____
- _____

CONFLICT – What is Jonah's conflict or choice in this story?

_____

_____

JUDGMENT – How do you judge Jonah?

_____

_____

EMOTION – Given everything above, what emotions are you aware of right now?

[ ] Mad   [ ] Sad   [ ] Glad   [ ] Fear   [ ] Shame

_____

_____

REFLECTION – Where in your own life do you hold similar judgments or have similar emotions?

_____

_____

APPLICATION – Given what you've just written, what do you want to happen in your life?

_____

_____

CONVICTION – Write down 2 or 3 things to take to God in prayer regarding what you've just written.

1. _____

2. _____

3. _____

ELIJAH IN FLIGHT
1 Kings 19:1-18

Elijah has had one of the best days in history! He challenged the 450 prophets of Baal to a contest of sacrifices, mocking them openly as they begged their god Baal to listen to their request for fire from heaven. When it came time for Elijah to pray to God for the fire to make his sacrifice, God sent fire from heaven consuming the sacrifice and overwhelming the altar.

Elijah defeated the prophets, and ultimately slaughtered them all. Then he prophesied the end of a three-year drought and outran a horse and chariot to escape the rainstorm that followed.

But great days like this produce great opposition. Jezebel, the wife of King Ahab had turned her wrathful gaze upon Elijah. When he killed the prophets of Baal, he also killed her prophets of Asherah. God's victory came at the expense of her majesty and reputation.

Things were about to take a turn for the worse as Elijah's euphoria collapsed and he was about to face a determined opponent who wanted him dead.

PRAY – Ask God to be present with you and to reveal Himself to you.

READ –Read 1 Kings 19:1-18, preferably out loud.

DATA – What pieces of data jump out of the story at you?

- _____

- _____

- _____

- _____

CONFLICT – What is Elijah's conflict or choice in this story?

_____

_____

JUDGMENT – How do you judge Elijah?

_____

_____

EMOTION – Given everything above, what emotions are you aware of right now?

[ ] Mad   [ ] Sad   [ ] Glad   [ ] Fear   [ ] Shame

_____

_____

REFLECTION – Where in your own life do you hold similar judgments or have similar emotions?

_____

_____

APPLICATION – Given what you've just written, what do you want to happen in your life?

_____

_____

CONVICTION – Write down 2 or 3 things to take to God in prayer regarding what you've just written.

1. _____

2. _____

3. _____

PETER AND THE UNCLEAN ANIMALS
Acts 10:1-48

The church which launched on the day of Pentecost was growing like crazy. God had been adding people to its numbers daily. The apostles were teaching and doing miracles in God's power in the streets of Jerusalem. Then the Jewish leaders resorted to extreme measures, killing Stephen, one of the first Deacons, and sent their firebrand enforcer Saul off to Damascus to find more believing Jews to arrest and torture.

The one common factor about the church at this point is that it was exclusively made up of Jewish men and women. All of the leaders and believers implicitly believed that the church was God's redemption of His covenant people, Israel. The gospel had never been presented to a Gentile, nor had any word of any Gentile believer reached the ears of the church.

Those in the church viewed the Gentiles as dirty and unclean. They were unworthy of attention or any social interaction. No self-respecting Jew, believing or unbelieving, would be caught socializing with a Gentile, let alone worshipping with one.

PRAY – Ask God to be present with you and to reveal Himself to you.

READ –Read Acts 10:1-48, preferably out loud.

DATA – What pieces of data jump out of the story at you?

*   _____

*   _____

*   _____

*   _____

CONFLICT – What is Peter's conflict or choice in this story?

_____

_____

JUDGMENT – How do you judge Peter?

_____

_____

EMOTION – Given everything above, what emotions are you aware of right now?

[ ] Mad   [ ] Sad   [ ] Glad   [ ] Fear   [ ] Shame

_____

_____

REFLECTION – Where in your own life do you hold similar judgments or have similar emotions?

_____

_____

APPLICATION – Given what you've just written, what do you want to happen in your life?

_____

_____

CONVICTION – Write down 2 or 3 things to take to God in prayer regarding what you've just written.

1. _____

2. _____

3. _____

DAVID LEARNS OF SAUL'S DEATH
2 Samuel 1:1-27

Saul, the King of Israel, took his own life rather than be captured by the Philistines when the battle turned against him. He knew they would torture and humiliate him if he was captured alive. He was wounded and could not fight free to save his own life. He asked his armor bearer to kill him, but the man refused, so Saul killed himself.

David had been running for his life to escape the hands of Saul for a long time. It became so bad that David was forced to ally himself with the Philistines for protection. David and his men were almost asked to fight in the battle against Saul, but at the last minute were sent back home.

When David returned to his home, he found that all the women and children of his settlement had been captured by Amalekite raiders while they were away. Immediately they set out to rescue their families – which they were able to do, destroying the band of raiders. Meanwhile, they were completely unaware of the results of the conflict between Saul and the Philistines.

PRAY – Ask God to be present with you and to reveal Himself to you.

READ –Read 2 Samuel 1:1-27, preferably out loud.

DATA – What pieces of data jump out of the story at you?

- _____
- _____
- _____
- _____

CONFLICT – What is David's conflict or choice in this story?

_____

_____

JUDGMENT – How do you judge David?

_____

_____

EMOTION – Given everything above, what emotions are you aware of right now?

[ ] Mad   [ ] Sad   [ ] Glad   [ ] Fear   [ ] Shame

_____

_____

REFLECTION – Where in your own life do you hold similar judgments or have similar emotions?

_____

_____

APPLICATION – Given what you've just written, what do you want to happen in your life?

_____

_____

CONVICTION – Write down 2 or 3 things to take to God in prayer regarding what you've just written.

1. _____

2. _____

3. _____

PAUL'S MIDNIGHT JAILBREAK
Acts 16:16-40

Paul and his missionary partner Silas were visiting the Roman colony at Philippi in Macedonia. They were on a missionary journey, visiting cities and preaching the good news and establishing churches of the people who believed. A few days earlier Paul had had a dream from God telling him to come to Macedonia and preach the gospel there. So they had come ready to see what God had in store for them.

Typically they first visited the Jewish synagogue in the city and delivered their message there. In the case of Philippi, they met a group of Jewish women who gathered by a river to worship. Many of them believed in Jesus. Paul and Silas were invited to the house of Lydia, a prominent woman who had believed and been baptized. They made Lydia's house their base of operation while they were in the city.

As they turned their attention to preaching to the Macedonian gentiles, they encountered opposition and persecution.

PRAY – Ask God to be present with you and to reveal Himself to you.

READ –Read Acts 16:16-40, preferably out loud.

DATA – What pieces of data jump out of the story at you?

- _____
- _____
- _____
- _____

CONFLICT – What is Paul's conflict or choice in this story?

_____

_____

JUDGMENT – How do you judge Paul?

_____

_____

EMOTION – Given everything above, what emotions are you aware of right now?

[ ] Mad   [ ] Sad   [ ] Glad   [ ] Fear   [ ] Shame

_____

_____

REFLECTION – Where in your own life do you hold similar judgments or have similar emotions?

_____

_____

APPLICATION – Given what you've just written, what do you want to happen in your life?

_____

_____

CONVICTION – Write down 2 or 3 things to take to God in prayer regarding what you've just written.

1. _____

2. _____

3. _____

OTHER BOOKS YOU MIGHT LIKE...

STUDY THE BIBLE: 6 EASY STEPS

Unsure how to study your Bible? Afraid you've been doing it wrong? Cut through the confusion with a simple approach that will get you on the right track!

Discover a study method anyone will understand and everyone can follow. Author Dennis Stevenson will show you an easy way to study your Bible so you can grow in your faith.

I am using the material to further help me understand what I read. It is making a tremendous difference!

--Maria

Study the Bible - Six Easy Steps shows you how to decide what to study, how to understand what it means and how you can apply the truth to your own life.

You'll find each step simply and clearly explained. Through helpful examples and guided exercises you'll gain insight into a deeper understanding of your Bible.

In *Study the Bible: Six Easy Steps* you'll discover:

- Three steps to draw life-changing application from your study
- Five words that reveal the meaning of the text
- How to use study Bibles, commentaries, and other resources
- A step-by-step approach to planning your next study
- A guided study that shows you how to put what you've learned into action

Study the Bible: Six Easy Steps is the guidebook you need to understand your Bible. If you like step-by-step learning, helpful examples, and guided exercises, then you'll appreciate Dennis Stevenson's easy-to-follow approach to studying God's word.

Available on Amazon.

JESUS ABOVE ALL: HOW WE VIEW JESUS SHAPES HOW WE WORSHIP HIM

Has worship lost its urgency? Do you long for worship that leaves you trembling and breathless? Discover the antidote for uninspired worship in an extraordinary vision of Jesus.

In this short book, Bible teacher and author Dennis Stevenson breathes fresh perspective into four familiar biblical encounters with Jesus and provides practical tools that will transform your daily worship. When you see Jesus clearly, your worship will never be the same again.

In this easy to read book you will find:

- 4 extraordinary encounters with Jesus that will shape your worship
- 3 simple worshipful practices you can start today
- Worship resources you can use to make these truths come to life every day

Jesus Above All is a quick read with long-lasting benefits. Dennis Stevenson's simple writing paints a vivid picture of the glory of God. If you like biblical stories, clear explanations, and practical application, you'll love this book.

Available on Amazon.

MEN IN THE BIBLE – SMALL GROUP STUDY GUIDE

A how-to manual designed for small group leaders who are looking for a Bible-based small group study that engages men's hearts. This book is for you if:

- You want to build a group of men who are open and vulnerable with one another.
- You want a study that can change men's lives without becoming overly academic.
- You want a study that feels "manly" without being macho.
- You want a study that extends a man's toolbox of life skills.
- You want to start a men's group but need a little guidance on the steps.

Men in the Bible uses a similar approach as this devotional guide and comes with a Getting Started Kit that provides small group leaders with all the resources they need to get started and lead a successful group.

Available as an e-book at your favorite retailer.

ABOUT THE AUTHOR

FOR MY DAY JOB, I design and implement computer software. I've been in multiple industries and really enjoy the intellectual and interpersonal challenges it brings. At the end of the day, I'm a writer. I share what I know so that others can benefit from it. If I'm not writing this book, I'll be writing another one soon. I live in the suburbs of Phoenix Arizona with my wife of 20+ years and two growing-up daughters. I'm not getting any younger, but I do hope to become wiser.

I'd love to connect with you! You can join my communication list at **www.dennis-stevenson.com/stay-in-touch** to learn about more books as they are published. This is the best way! But you can also follow me online on Twitter at **@AuthorDCSJr** or my author page on Facebook at **AuthorDennisStevenson**.

Printed in Great Britain
by Amazon

20725405R00058